Explanation of Smart Cities and Their Significance

Smart cities are urban areas that utilize digital technology and data to enhance the quality of life for their residents, improve the efficiency of urban services, and promote sustainability. These cities integrate information and communication technology (ICT) and the Internet of Things (IoT) to manage resources more effectively and provide better services. The significance of smart cities lies in their ability to address the complex challenges faced by modern urban areas, such as population growth, traffic congestion, energy consumption, and environmental sustainability.

A smart city leverages technology to create a more interconnected and responsive urban environment. For instance, sensors and data analytics can monitor air quality in real-time, enabling city officials to take immediate action to reduce pollution. Similarly, smart transportation systems can optimize traffic flow, reducing commute times and lowering carbon emissions. By embracing these technological advancements, smart cities aim to create a more efficient, sustainable, and livable urban experience for their inhabitants.

Overview of the Integration of Digital Technology and Data in Urban Planning:

The integration of digital technology and data in urban planning is at the core of smart city development. This involves the deployment of various technologies such as IoT devices, artificial intelligence (AI), and big data analytics to collect, analyze, and utilize data for decision-making processes. In smart cities, data from multiple sources—such as traffic cameras, weather sensors, and social media—are aggregated and analyzed to provide insights that can improve city operations and enhance the quality of life for residents.

For example, digital technology can be used to create smart grids that optimize energy distribution and consumption, reducing waste and lowering energy costs. Smart water management systems can detect leaks and monitor water quality, ensuring a reliable and safe water supply. In urban planning, data analytics can help city planners design more efficient public transportation systems, identify areas in need of infrastructure improvements, and create more effective disaster response plans. The seamless integration of digital technology and data in urban planning is essential for building smart cities that are resilient, sustainable, and responsive to the needs of their residents.

Importance of Smart Cities

Benefits of Smart Cities for Urban Living:

Smart cities offer numerous benefits for urban living, making them highly attractive to residents, businesses, and governments. One of the most significant benefits is the improvement in quality of life. By utilizing technology to optimize city services, smart cities can provide cleaner air, safer streets, and more efficient public transportation. For example, smart street lighting can adjust brightness based on the presence of pedestrians and vehicles, enhancing safety while conserving energy.

Another key benefit is the enhancement of economic opportunities. Smart cities attract businesses and investors by offering advanced infrastructure and a tech-savvy environment. They also create new job opportunities in the technology and data analysis sectors. Moreover, smart cities promote social inclusion by providing digital services that are accessible to all residents, regardless of their socioeconomic status.

The Role of Technology in Creating Sustainable, Efficient, and Livable Environments:

Technology plays a pivotal role in creating sustainable, efficient, and livable environments in smart cities. Sustainable urban development is achieved using renewable energy sources, smart grids, and energy-efficient buildings. For instance, smart buildings equipped with sensors can automatically adjust heating, cooling, and lighting to reduce energy consumption, contributing to a city's overall sustainability goals.

Efficiency is another cornerstone of smart cities. Advanced technologies such as AI and machine learning can optimize various city functions, from traffic management to waste collection. For example, AI-driven traffic management systems can reduce congestion and minimize travel times by dynamically adjusting traffic signals based on real-time data. This not only improves efficiency but also reduces the environmental impact of transportation.

Lastly, technology enhances livability by providing residents with better access to services and improving their overall experience of the city. Smart healthcare systems can offer telemedicine services, making healthcare more accessible and reducing the burden on hospitals. Mobile apps can provide real-time information on public transportation, helping residents plan their commutes more effectively. By leveraging technology, smart cities can create environments that are not only efficient and sustainable but also more enjoyable and convenient for their inhabitants.

Smart cities represent the future of urban living, where technology and data are harnessed to create better, more sustainable, and livable environments. Through the integration of digital technology in urban planning and the myriad benefits it brings, smart cities are poised to address the challenges of modern urbanization and improve the quality of life for people around the world.

Key Components of Smart Cities

Infrastructure:

Smart buildings are a fundamental component of smart city infrastructure, designed to optimize resource usage and enhance the living experience through advanced technology. These buildings are equipped with IoT devices, sensors, and automation systems that monitor and control various parameters such as temperature, lighting, and energy consumption. For instance, a smart building might use motion sensors to adjust lighting and HVAC systems based on occupancy, thereby reducing energy waste and improving comfort. Additionally, smart construction techniques involve the use of sustainable materials and construction methods that minimize environmental impact and enhance the durability and efficiency of buildings.

Intelligent Transportation Systems:

Intelligent transportation systems (ITS) are crucial for managing urban mobility and reducing traffic congestion. These systems leverage real-time data and advanced algorithms to optimize traffic flow, improve public transit services, and enhance road safety. For example, adaptive traffic signals can adjust their timing based on traffic conditions, reducing wait times and improving fuel efficiency. Similarly, smart parking solutions can guide drivers to available parking spots, decreasing the time spent searching for parking and reducing traffic congestion.

IoT-enabled Utilities and Services:

IoT-enabled utilities and services are essential for creating efficient and sustainable urban environments. These systems use connected sensors and devices to monitor and manage utilities such as water, electricity, and waste management. For example, smart water meters can detect leaks and monitor water usage in real time, helping to conserve water and reduce costs. IoT-enabled waste management systems can optimize collection routes based on bin fill levels, reducing operational costs and minimizing the environmental impact of waste collection.

Transportation:

Autonomous and connected vehicles are transforming urban transportation by enhancing safety, efficiency, and convenience. Autonomous vehicles use advanced sensors, AI, and machine learning algorithms to navigate and operate without human intervention. These vehicles can communicate with each other and with traffic infrastructure to optimize routes, reduce traffic jams, and minimize the risk of accidents. Connected vehicles, on the other hand, are equipped with internet connectivity that allows them to share data with other vehicles and infrastructure, improving traffic management and providing real-time information to drivers.

Smart Traffic Management Systems:

Smart traffic management systems are designed to improve traffic flow and reduce congestion using advanced technologies. These systems collect and analyze data from various sources, including traffic cameras, sensors, and GPS devices, to make real-time adjustments to traffic signals and provide drivers with up-to-date information on traffic conditions. For instance, AI-powered traffic control systems can predict traffic patterns and adjust signal timings accordingly, reducing delays and improving the overall efficiency of the transportation network.

Public Transportation Improvements and Integration:

Public transportation improvements and integration are essential for creating sustainable and efficient urban mobility solutions. Smart cities invest in modernizing public transit systems with technologies such as real-time tracking, mobile payment options, and integrated transportation networks. For example, real-time tracking allows passengers to receive accurate information on bus and train arrival times, improving the reliability and convenience of public transportation.

Integration of various modes of transportation, such as buses, trains, and bike-sharing services, ensures seamless connectivity and encourages the use of public transit over private vehicles.

Energy Management:

Smart grids are advanced energy distribution networks that utilize digital technology to manage the production, distribution, and consumption of electricity more efficiently. These grids can integrate renewable energy sources such as solar and wind power, ensuring a stable and sustainable energy supply. For example, smart grids can balance energy demand and supply by automatically adjusting the flow of electricity based on real-time data from sensors and meters. This capability allows for the efficient integration of renewable energy sources, reducing reliance on fossil fuels and lowering carbon emissions.

Energy-efficient Buildings and Infrastructure:

Energy-efficient buildings and infrastructure are key to reducing the environmental impact of urban areas. Smart cities implement energy-saving technologies and practices in building design, construction, and operation. For instance, buildings can be equipped with smart HVAC systems that adjust heating and cooling based on occupancy and weather conditions, significantly reducing energy consumption. Additionally, the use of energy-efficient materials and construction techniques can further enhance the sustainability of urban infrastructure.

Demand Response and Energy Storage Solutions:

Demand response and energy storage solutions play a crucial role in balancing energy demand and supply in smart cities. Demand response programs incentivize consumers to reduce or shift their energy usage during peak times, helping to alleviate pressure on the grid and reduce energy costs. Energy storage solutions, such as batteries, allow excess energy generated from renewable sources to be stored and used when demand is high or supply is low. These technologies ensure a reliable and resilient energy supply, supporting the sustainability goals of smart cities.

Public Services:

Digital government services are a cornerstone of smart cities, providing residents with efficient and accessible public services through online platforms. These services include e-governance portals, digital identity systems, and online service delivery for tasks such as paying bills, applying for permits, and accessing public records. For example, a digital identity system allows citizens to securely access government services online, reducing the need for physical visits to government offices and streamlining administrative processes.

Smart Healthcare Systems:

Smart healthcare systems leverage technology to improve the delivery and accessibility of healthcare services. These systems include telemedicine platforms, electronic health records (EHRs), and remote monitoring devices. Telemedicine platforms enable patients to consult with healthcare providers remotely, increasing access to medical care and reducing the burden on healthcare facilities. EHRs provide healthcare professionals with real-time access to patient information, enhancing the quality and efficiency of care. Remote monitoring devices allow patients to manage chronic conditions from home, reducing hospital visits and improving health outcomes.

Enhanced Public Safety and Emergency Response:

Enhanced public safety and emergency response are critical components of smart cities, ensuring the well-being of residents through advanced technology and data analytics. Smart cities deploy surveillance cameras, sensors, and communication networks to monitor public spaces and detect potential threats. For instance, AI-powered video analytics can identify suspicious activities and alert authorities in real time, enabling prompt intervention. Additionally, integrated emergency response systems use data from various sources to coordinate and optimize emergency services, reducing response times and improving the effectiveness of interventions during crises.

The key components of smart cities—advanced infrastructure, intelligent transportation, efficient energy management, and enhanced public services—work together to create urban environments that are sustainable, efficient, and highly livable. By leveraging technology and data, smart cities can address the challenges of modern urbanization and improve the quality of life for their residents, paving the way for a more connected and resilient future.

Technology Enablers for Smart Cities

The Internet of Things (IoT) is a foundational technology for smart cities, enabling the connection of devices, systems, and services that can communicate and exchange data. By embedding sensors and actuators in everyday objects and infrastructure, IoT creates a network of interconnected devices that collect and share information in real time. This connectivity allows for seamless integration and coordination of various city functions, from traffic management to energy distribution. For example, IoT-enabled streetlights can adjust their brightness based on pedestrian and vehicular traffic, conserving energy and enhancing public safety.

Examples of IoT Applications in Smart Cities:

IoT applications in smart cities are diverse and impactful, enhancing efficiency, sustainability, and quality of life. Smart waste management systems, for instance, use IoT sensors to monitor the fill levels of garbage bins and optimize collection routes, reducing operational costs and environmental impact. In the realm of public safety, IoT-enabled surveillance cameras and sensors can detect unusual activities and alert authorities in real time, improving response times and crime prevention. Additionally, smart water management systems can use IoT sensors to monitor water quality and detect leaks, ensuring a safe and reliable water supply for residents.

Big Data and Analytics:

Big data and analytics are crucial for the functioning of smart cities, as they enable the collection, processing, and interpretation of vast amounts of data generated by IoT devices and other sources. This data provides valuable insights into various aspects of urban life, from traffic patterns to energy consumption. By analyzing this data, city planners and managers can make informed decisions that enhance the efficiency and sustainability of urban services. For example, data analytics can help identify peak traffic times and optimize public transportation schedules accordingly, reducing congestion and improving commuter experiences.

How Big Data Drives Decision-Making in Smart Cities:

Big data drives decision-making in smart cities by providing a comprehensive and detailed understanding of urban dynamics. Advanced analytics techniques, such as machine learning and predictive modeling, can identify trends and patterns that inform policy and planning decisions. For instance, predictive analytics can forecast energy demand based on historical consumption data and weather patterns, enabling utilities to manage supply more effectively. Similarly, big data can be used to assess the impact of environmental policies, track pollution levels, and develop strategies to improve air quality and public health.

Artificial Intelligence (AI):

Artificial Intelligence (AI) plays a transformative role in urban management, automating processes and enhancing the decision-making capabilities of city officials. AI applications in smart cities range from traffic control to waste management. For example, AI-powered traffic management systems can analyze real-time data from traffic sensors and cameras to optimize signal timings, reducing congestion and improving traffic flow. In waste management, AI algorithms can predict waste generation patterns and optimize collection schedules, minimizing costs and environmental impact.

Predictive Analytics and Machine Learning for City Planning:

Predictive analytics and machine learning are key AI technologies that drive smart city planning and operations. By analyzing historical and real-time data, these technologies can forecast future trends and help city planners make proactive decisions. For instance, machine learning models can predict the impact of new infrastructure projects on traffic and public transportation, allowing planners to design more efficient and effective urban layouts. Additionally, predictive analytics can identify areas at risk of flooding or other natural disasters, enabling cities to implement preventive measures and enhance resilience.

5G and Connectivity:

The advent of 5G technology is a game-changer for smart city infrastructure, providing the high-speed, low-latency connectivity needed to support a vast array of IoT devices and applications. 5G networks can handle large volumes of data with minimal delay, enabling real-time communication and control of smart city systems. This enhanced connectivity supports the deployment of advanced technologies such as autonomous vehicles, smart grids, and remote healthcare services, making cities more efficient and responsive to the needs of their residents.

Enhanced Connectivity for Real-Time Data Transmission

Enhanced connectivity provided by 5G technology is essential for real-time data transmission, which is critical for the functioning of smart cities. With 5G, data from sensors, cameras, and other IoT devices can be transmitted instantaneously, allowing for real-time monitoring and management of city services. For example, real-time data transmission enables dynamic traffic management, where traffic signals and routes can be adjusted based on current conditions, reducing congestion and travel times. In emergency response, 5G connectivity allows for rapid communication and coordination between first responders, improving the efficiency and effectiveness of their operations.

The technology enablers for smart cities—IoT, big data and analytics, AI, and 5G connectivity—work together to create a highly interconnected and intelligent urban environment. These technologies provide the tools and capabilities needed to manage the complexities of modern urban life, enhancing the efficiency, sustainability, and livability of cities. By leveraging these advancements, smart cities can address the challenges of urbanization and improve the quality of life for their residents, setting the stage for a more connected and resilient future.

Case Studies of Smart Cities

Overview of Singapore's Smart City Initiatives:

Singapore is widely recognized as a global leader in smart city development, thanks to its comprehensive and forward-thinking approach. The city-state's Smart Nation initiative, launched in 2014, aims to harness technology to improve urban living, drive economic growth, and create a sustainable environment. This initiative encompasses various sectors, including healthcare, transportation, and public services, leveraging digital technology and data analytics to enhance efficiency and quality of life.

Key Projects and Their Impact on Urban Living:

One of the standout projects under Singapore's Smart Nation initiative is the Smart Health Assist program. This program uses telemedicine and remote monitoring to provide healthcare services to residents, particularly the elderly, in their homes. By equipping patients with wearable devices that monitor vital signs, healthcare providers can track health conditions in real-time and intervene when necessary, reducing hospital visits and improving patient outcomes.

Another significant project is the deployment of the Intelligent Transport System (ITS). This system includes smart traffic lights, electronic road pricing, and real-time traffic information to manage congestion and optimize traffic flow. For example, the Green Link Determining (GLIDE) system adjusts traffic signal timings based on real-time traffic conditions, reducing wait times and improving fuel efficiency. These initiatives have significantly enhanced the efficiency of Singapore's transportation network, making commuting more convenient and reducing environmental impact.

Barcelona's Approach to Smart City Development:

Barcelona's smart city development is characterized by a holistic and citizen-centric approach. The city has implemented a series of initiatives aimed at improving urban services, enhancing sustainability, and fostering innovation. Barcelona's City Protocol Society framework guides its smart city strategy, emphasizing collaboration between government, businesses, and citizens to co-create solutions for urban challenges.

Innovations and Technologies Implemented:

Barcelona has implemented several innovative technologies to transform urban living. One notable example is the city's smart lighting system. This system uses IoT sensors to adjust streetlight brightness based on pedestrian and vehicular traffic, reducing energy consumption and improving public safety. Additionally, the city has introduced smart waste management solutions, where sensors in waste containers monitor fill levels and optimize collection routes, reducing costs and environmental impact.

Another groundbreaking project is the 22@Barcelona innovation district, which has transformed a former industrial area into a hub for technology and knowledge-based industries. This district features high-speed internet connectivity, smart buildings, and sustainable infrastructure, attracting startups and tech companies. By fostering an ecosystem of innovation, Barcelona is driving economic growth and creating job opportunities in cutting-edge industries.

Amsterdam's Smart City Strategy:

Amsterdam's smart city strategy is built on the principles of sustainability, innovation, and collaboration. The city has established the Amsterdam Smart City (ASC) platform, which brings together government, businesses, and citizens to co-create smart solutions. This collaborative approach ensures that the initiatives implemented are aligned with the needs and priorities of the community, fostering greater engagement and ownership.

Successful Projects and Future Plans:

One of Amsterdam's most successful smart city projects is the City-zen initiative, which focuses on creating energy-efficient neighborhoods. This project includes the installation of smart grids, energy storage systems, and sustainable building technologies to reduce energy consumption and promote the use of renewable energy sources. For example, the De Ceuvel neighborhood has transformed a polluted industrial site into a sustainable urban oasis, featuring solar panels, green roofs, and innovative water management systems.

Amsterdam is also a pioneer in smart mobility solutions. The city has implemented a comprehensive network of electric vehicle (EV) charging stations, promoting the adoption of EVs and reducing carbon emissions. Additionally, the Smart Traffic Management system uses real-time data to optimize traffic flow and reduce congestion. This system includes dynamic traffic signals, smart parking solutions, and integrated public transportation networks, making commuting more efficient and environmentally friendly.

Looking to the future, Amsterdam plans to expand its smart city initiatives to further enhance sustainability and livability. Upcoming projects include the development of smart grids for energy distribution, the deployment of more IoT-enabled devices for real-time data collection, and the promotion of circular economy practices to minimize waste and resource consumption.

The case studies of Singapore, Barcelona, and Amsterdam illustrate the diverse approaches and innovative solutions that smart cities can adopt to improve urban living. These cities have leveraged technology and data to create more efficient, sustainable, and livable environments, setting a benchmark for other cities around the world. By learning from these examples, other urban areas can develop their own smart city strategies to address the challenges of modern urbanization and enhance the quality of life for their residents.

Challenges and Solutions in Developing Smart Cities

Technical Challenges:

One of the primary technical challenges in developing smart cities is ensuring compatibility and integration across diverse infrastructure systems. Smart cities rely on a complex network of interconnected devices and systems, including transportation, energy, water, and waste management. Integrating these systems can be difficult due to differences in technology standards, legacy infrastructure, and varying levels of technological maturity. For instance, upgrading an existing city's infrastructure to support smart grids and IoT devices requires significant coordination and investment, as older systems may not be designed to interface with modern technologies.

Cybersecurity and Data Privacy Concerns:

As smart cities become more reliant on digital technology and data, cybersecurity and data privacy concerns become increasingly critical. The vast amount of data collected by smart city systems, such as personal information from residents and operational data from city services, presents a lucrative target for cybercriminals. Ensuring the security of this data requires robust cybersecurity measures, including encryption, secure communication protocols, and regular vulnerability assessments. Additionally, protecting residents' privacy is essential, necessitating the implementation of strict data governance policies and transparent data usage practices to build public trust.

Economic Challenges:

Funding and investment are significant economic challenges in the development of smart cities. Implementing smart city initiatives requires substantial financial resources for technology deployment, infrastructure upgrades, and ongoing maintenance. Securing funding from public budgets can be challenging, especially in cities with limited financial resources or competing priorities. Additionally, attracting private investment may be difficult without clear financial returns or proven success models. Cities must develop innovative financing strategies, such as public-private partnerships, to overcome these financial hurdles and ensure the sustainability of smart city projects.

Cost-Benefit Analysis of Smart City Technologies:

Conducting a cost-benefit analysis of smart city technologies is essential to justify investments and prioritize projects. This analysis involves assessing the upfront costs of implementing smart technologies against the long-term benefits, such as operational efficiencies, cost savings, and improved quality of life for residents. For example, while installing smart meters for water and electricity may require significant initial investment, the long-term benefits of reduced resource consumption and lower utility costs can offset these expenses. Cities must carefully evaluate the potential return on investment for each project to ensure that resources are allocated effectively.

Social Challenges:

The digital divide and unequal access to technology present significant social challenges in developing smart cities. Ensuring that all residents have access to the benefits of smart city initiatives requires addressing disparities in technology availability, affordability, and digital literacy. For instance, lower-income communities may lack access to high-speed internet or smart devices, limiting their ability to participate in and benefit from smart city services. Cities must implement inclusive policies and initiatives, such as providing affordable internet access and digital literacy programs, to bridge the digital divide and promote equitable access to technology.

Public Acceptance and Engagement:

Public acceptance and engagement are crucial for the success of smart city initiatives. Residents may be skeptical of new technologies or concerned about privacy and security implications. Building public trust and support requires transparent communication, community involvement, and education. Cities must engage with residents through public consultations, workshops, and information campaigns to explain the benefits of smart city projects and address any concerns. Involving the community in the planning and implementation process can foster a sense of ownership and increase the likelihood of successful adoption.

Solutions and Best Practices:

Public-private partnerships (PPPs) are a vital solution for overcoming funding and implementation challenges in smart city development. By partnering with private sector companies, cities can leverage additional financial resources, technical expertise, and innovative solutions. For example, a city might collaborate with technology firms to develop and deploy smart infrastructure, sharing the costs and benefits of the project. PPPs can also facilitate the transfer of knowledge and best practices, helping cities to implement smart city initiatives more efficiently and effectively.

Policy Frameworks and Regulatory Support:

Establishing robust policy frameworks and regulatory support is essential for the successful development of smart cities. Governments must create clear policies and regulations that promote innovation, protect data privacy, and ensure cybersecurity. For instance, data protection laws should mandate stringent data handling practices, while regulatory frameworks should encourage the deployment of new technologies. Additionally, providing incentives such as tax breaks or grants can stimulate investment in smart city projects. Effective policy and regulatory support can create a conducive environment for the growth and sustainability of smart cities.

Community Involvement and Education:

Community involvement and education are key to fostering public acceptance and ensuring the success of smart city initiatives. Engaging residents in the planning and decision-making process helps to address their concerns and build trust. Cities can organize workshops, town hall meetings, and pilot projects to gather feedback and involve the community in shaping smart city solutions. Additionally, educational programs that enhance digital literacy and awareness can empower residents to make the most of smart city technologies. By promoting a culture of innovation and inclusivity, cities can ensure that smart city initiatives benefit all residents.

Developing smart cities involves navigating a range of technical, economic, and social challenges. By leveraging solutions such as public-private partnerships, robust policy frameworks, and community involvement, cities can overcome these obstacles and create urban environments that are efficient, sustainable, and inclusive. Addressing these challenges and implementing best practices is crucial for the successful realization of smart city visions, ultimately enhancing the quality of life for residents and paving the way for a more connected and resilient future.

Future Trends in Smart Cities

Sustainable Urban Development:

As cities strive to become more sustainable, green building technologies will play a crucial role in future urban development. These technologies encompass a range of practices and materials aimed at reducing the environmental impact of buildings. For instance, energy-efficient HVAC systems, solar panels, and green roofs can significantly decrease a building's carbon footprint. Advanced materials like self-healing concrete and smart glass that adjusts transparency based on sunlight exposure further enhance the sustainability of urban structures. By integrating these technologies, cities can create buildings that are not only environmentally friendly but also cost-effective in the long run, reducing energy consumption and operational costs.

Urban Agriculture and Green Spaces:

Urban agriculture and green spaces are becoming increasingly important for promoting sustainability and enhancing the quality of life in cities. Urban farms and rooftop gardens provide fresh, locally grown produce, reducing the need for transportation and lowering carbon emissions. Green spaces such as parks, community gardens, and green roofs offer numerous benefits, including improving air quality, reducing urban heat island effects, and providing recreational areas for residents. These initiatives also support biodiversity and contribute to the overall resilience of urban ecosystems. By prioritizing urban agriculture and green spaces, cities can foster healthier environments and more sustainable food systems.

Smart Mobility:

The future of urban mobility will be heavily influenced by innovations in electric and autonomous vehicles. Electric vehicles (EVs) are crucial for reducing greenhouse gas emissions and improving air quality in cities. Advances in battery technology and charging infrastructure are making EVs more accessible and practical for urban use. Autonomous vehicles (AVs), equipped with advanced sensors and AI, have the potential to revolutionize transportation by reducing traffic congestion, minimizing accidents, and optimizing route efficiency. For example, autonomous ride-sharing services can provide convenient and affordable transportation options, reducing the need for private car ownership and alleviating pressure on urban infrastructure.

Integrated Mobility Platforms:

Integrated mobility platforms will be key to creating seamless and efficient transportation systems in smart cities. These platforms combine various modes of transportation—such as buses, trains, bicycles, and ride-sharing services—into a unified network that can be accessed through a single app or platform. By providing real-time information on schedules, routes, and availability, integrated mobility platforms enable residents to plan their journeys more efficiently and choose the most convenient and sustainable modes of transport. This integration promotes the use of public transit and reduces reliance on private vehicles, contributing to lower traffic congestion and environmental impact.

Health and Well-being:

Smart healthcare systems and telemedicine will play a vital role in improving health and well-being in future smart cities. These systems leverage digital technologies to provide more accessible, efficient, and personalized healthcare services. Telemedicine platforms enable remote consultations with healthcare providers, reducing the need for physical visits to medical facilities and increasing access to care, especially for those in underserved areas. Wearable devices and IoT-enabled health monitoring systems can track vital signs and alert medical professionals to potential health issues in real time. By integrating these technologies, cities can enhance the quality of healthcare and promote preventive care practices.

Urban Design for Healthy Living:

Urban design that prioritizes health and well-being is essential for creating livable and vibrant cities. This includes designing pedestrian-friendly streets, promoting active transportation such as walking and cycling, and ensuring access to green spaces and recreational facilities. Urban planners can incorporate elements such as wide sidewalks, dedicated bike lanes, and public parks to encourage physical activity and reduce reliance on motor vehicles. Additionally, implementing policies that limit air pollution and ensure clean water and sanitation can further enhance residents' health. By focusing on healthy urban design, cities can create environments that support physical and mental well-being.

Resilience and Adaptability

Future smart cities will need to be resilient and adaptable to effectively manage disasters and emergencies. Advanced technologies such as

AI, IoT, and big data analytics can enhance disaster management and emergency response capabilities. For example, AI algorithms can predict natural disasters such as floods and earthquakes by analyzing historical data and real-time sensor information. IoT devices can monitor environmental conditions and provide early warnings to residents and authorities. During emergencies, integrated communication systems can coordinate response efforts and ensure timely dissemination of information. These technologies enable cities to respond more quickly and effectively to disasters, minimizing damage and protecting lives.

Adaptive Infrastructure for Climate Change:

Climate change poses significant challenges for urban infrastructure, requiring cities to develop adaptive and resilient solutions. Adaptive infrastructure is designed to withstand and respond to changing environmental conditions, such as rising sea levels, extreme weather events, and temperature fluctuations. For instance, flood-resistant buildings and permeable pavements can help manage stormwater and reduce the risk of flooding. Green infrastructure, such as urban forests and wetlands, can mitigate the impacts of heat waves and improve air quality. By investing in adaptive infrastructure, cities can enhance their resilience to climate change and ensure the long-term sustainability of their urban environments.

The future trends in smart cities will be driven by advancements in sustainable urban development, smart mobility, health and well-being, and resilience. By embracing green building technologies, promoting urban agriculture, and leveraging innovations in transportation and healthcare, cities can create more livable and sustainable environments. Furthermore, developing adaptive infrastructure and enhancing disaster management capabilities will be crucial for addressing the challenges posed by climate change. By staying at the forefront of these trends, smart cities can improve the quality of life for their residents and build a more resilient and sustainable future.

Summary and Future Outlook

Summary of Key Points:

Smart cities represent the future of urban living, leveraging technology and data to create more efficient, sustainable, and livable environments. The benefits of smart cities are multifaceted, including enhanced quality of life for residents, improved economic opportunities, and greater environmental sustainability. Key components of smart cities include advanced infrastructure such as smart buildings and intelligent transportation systems, IoT-enabled utilities and services, and comprehensive energy management systems. These elements work together to optimize urban operations, reduce resource consumption, and provide better services to residents.

Smart cities also prioritize public services, integrating digital government services, smart healthcare systems, and enhanced public safety measures. By using real-time data and advanced technologies, smart cities can respond more effectively to the needs of their populations, ensuring safer, healthier, and more connected communities. Additionally, smart city initiatives focus on fostering social inclusion, bridging the digital divide, and ensuring that all residents benefit from technological advancements.

Importance of Technology and Innovation in Urban Development:

Technology and innovation are at the heart of smart city development. The integration of IoT, big data, AI, and 5G connectivity enables cities to collect and analyze vast amounts of data, driving informed decision-making and optimizing urban operations. For example, AI-powered traffic management systems can reduce congestion and improve transportation efficiency, while smart grids and renewable energy sources enhance sustainability and resilience.

Innovation also plays a critical role in addressing the challenges of urbanization, such as population growth, environmental degradation, and resource scarcity. By adopting cutting-edge technologies and innovative solutions, cities can create more adaptive and resilient infrastructures, promote sustainable development, and improve the overall quality of life for their residents. The continuous evolution of technology will further enhance the capabilities of smart cities, enabling them to meet the changing needs of urban populations and create more sustainable and livable environments.

Future Outlook:

The potential for smart cities to transform urban living is immense. As technology continues to advance, smart cities will become more efficient, sustainable, and responsive to the needs of their residents. Innovations in areas such as autonomous vehicles, renewable energy, and digital healthcare will revolutionize urban services, making cities safer, cleaner, and more convenient places to live. For instance, the widespread adoption of electric and autonomous vehicles will reduce traffic congestion and emissions, while smart healthcare systems will provide more accessible and personalized care.

Smart cities will also foster economic growth by attracting businesses and investments in technology and innovation sectors. By creating an environment that supports entrepreneurship and innovation, smart cities can drive job creation and economic development, benefiting both residents and businesses. Furthermore, the integration of smart technologies will enhance social inclusion and equity, ensuring that all residents have access to the benefits of urban development.

The Ongoing Evolution and Future Prospects of Smart Cities:

The evolution of smart cities is an ongoing process, driven by continuous advancements in technology and changing urban dynamics. As cities continue to grow and face new challenges, the development of smart solutions will be essential to addressing these issues and creating sustainable urban environments. The future prospects of smart cities are promising, with emerging technologies such as AI, IoT, and 5G poised to further enhance urban living.

In the coming years, we can expect to see more cities adopting smart city initiatives and integrating advanced technologies into their infrastructure and services. The development of adaptive infrastructure and resilient systems will be critical in addressing the impacts of climate change and ensuring the long-term sustainability of urban environments. Additionally, the increasing emphasis on community involvement and collaboration will ensure that smart city initiatives are inclusive and reflective of the needs and priorities of residents.

Smart cities have the potential to transform urban living by leveraging technology and innovation to create more efficient, sustainable, and livable environments. The ongoing evolution of smart cities will be shaped by continuous advancements in technology, the integration of innovative solutions, and a focus on social inclusion and sustainability. By embracing these trends, cities can improve the quality of life for their residents and build a more connected and resilient future.

References

1. Hollands, R. G. (2008). "Will the real smart city please stand up? Intelligent, progressive or entrepreneurial?" City, 12(3), 303-320.

2. Caragliu, A., Del Bo, C., & Nijkamp, P. (2011). "Smart Cities in Europe." Journal of Urban Technology, 18(2), 65-82.

3. Chourabi, H., Nam, T., Walker, S., Gil-Garcia, J. R., Mellouli, S., Nahon, K., ... & Scholl, H. J. (2012). "Understanding Smart Cities: An Integrative Framework." 45th Hawaii International Conference on System Sciences, 2289-2297.

4. Kitchin, R. (2014). "The real-time city? Big data and smart urbanism." GeoJournal, 79(1), 1-14.

5. Townsend, A. M. (2013). Smart Cities: Big Data, Civic Hackers, and the Quest for a New Utopia. W.W. Norton & Company.

6. Batty, M., Axhausen, K. W., Giannotti, F., Pozdnoukhov, A., Bazzani, A., Wachowicz, M., ... & Portugali, Y. (2012). "Smart cities of the future." The European Physical Journal Special Topics, 214(1), 481-518.

7. Nam, T., & Pardo, T. A. (2011). "Conceptualizing smart city with dimensions of technology, people, and institutions." Proceedings of the 12th Annual International Digital Government Research Conference: Digital Government Innovation in Challenging Times, 282-291.

8. Zanella, A., Bui, N., Castellani, A., Vangelista, L., & Zorzi, M. (2014). "Internet of Things for Smart Cities." IEEE Internet of Things Journal, 1(1), 22-32.

9. Schaffers, H., Komninos, N., Pallot, M., Trousse, B., Nilsson, M., & Oliveira, A. (2011). "Smart Cities and the Future Internet: Towards Cooperation Frameworks for Open Innovation." The Future Internet Assembly, 431-446.

10. European Commission. (2013). "Smart Cities and Communities: Strategic Implementation Plan." European Innovation Partnership on Smart Cities and Communities.

11. Giffinger, R., Fertner, C., Kramar, H., Kalasek, R., Pichler-Milanović, N., & Meijers, E. (2007). "Smart Cities: Ranking of European Medium-Sized Cities." Centre of Regional Science, Vienna University of Technology.

12. Cohen, B. (2015). "The 3 Generations of Smart Cities." Fast Company.

13. Sikora-Fernandez, D. (2018). "Smarter cities: trends, challenges, and opportunities in

the city's business and innovation ecosystem."
Cities, 72, 43-51.

14. Alawadhi, S., & Scholl, H. J. (2016).
"Smart governance: A cross-case analysis of
smart city initiatives." Proceedings of the 49th
Hawaii International Conference on System
Sciences.

15. Kumar, P., & Dahiya, B. (2017). "Smart
cities and environmental sustainability: An
empirical study based on emerging
economies." Journal of Cleaner Production,
189, 725-734.

These references provide a comprehensive
foundation for understanding the various
aspects of smart cities, including their
development, technologies, challenges, and
future prospects. For further reading, these
sources offer detailed insights and case
studies on the transformative potential of
smart cities in the digital age.

www.ingramcontent.com/pod-product-compliance
Lightning Source LLC
Chambersburg PA
CBHW030036230526
45472CB00002B/539